Winning

THE LOTTERY

of the Mind

"When You Seize an Opportunity it creates more opportunities"

John D. Rockefeller

You are holding the opportunity

Winning
THE LOTTERY
of the Mind

Stephen R. Beebe

authorHOUSE®

AuthorHouse™
1663 Liberty Drive
Bloomington, IN 47403
www.authorhouse.com
Phone: 1-800-839-8640

First published by AuthorHouse   05/19/2011

ISBN: 978-1-4634-0985-2 (sc)
ISBN: 978-1-4634-0983-8 (ebk)

Library of Congress Control Number: 2011908626

Printed in the United States of America

Dedication:

To my son Gary

Forward

By Robert Burns

It was my privilege to find myself at my rock-bottom. Do not misunderstand me here. It was a world of pain, and there appeared to be no way out. Then I drew some very smart friends around me and we began to work on it, for all of our sakes.

Over the course of the work, my life began to turn around, and I found that as long as there is breath, there is hope.

Now if you have hope, the next thing that you need is a direction. This is the reason that we are stressing the finding of your passion, then making a plan, and then getting to work.

I have become a very big fan of celebrating your successes, and then getting back to work. It is my privilege to tell you that if you have ever come to a place where you wished that you could get a do-over in life, well here it is.

What follows are the best tips ever on how to take a life that is down, and bring it back up again to make it flourish. I know very well that if I can do it, so can you. This is your do-over in life. Take it.

Robert A. Burns

Introduction

In our lives from bad programming, grief often besets us. We mention some in this work, but what you are about to read is something that goes well beyond anything ever published in either the religious press, or in the secular self help industry because the focus of this work is the Human Potential Movement.

What is the extent of a human's real and innate abilities? These things are beyond the scope of the common imagination.

They are phenomenal!

Consider this. If your computer was down, your hard drive had crashed. Then someone representing himself as a computer repairperson came to you. This person would say something like "I can help you with your hard drive, but I have no idea how a computer works," Would you allow him to work on your computer? I do not think so! And, yet for some reason we allow the psychiatric community which admittedly has only a minimal knowledge of how the mind works full license to be in full charge of the issues of our minds. Why?

You should hold no quarter for them in terms of healing, because they focus toward management of the condition rather than healing it. Therefore, in the matters of corporate medicine, we ought to come down on the side of the healers, and not so much the business end of it all.

When you are talking about matters of human potential, talking about money seems almost to profane the issue. Those who treat the human potential as something that is purely technical, miss the boat. You should know that people are far more than spiraling coils of self-replicating D.N.A.

We are spiritual beings having a physical experience. Then we see that the spirit is that sentient part that makes you into you, and that fleshy part is so much of an envelope encasing that sentient part.

The brain is the mechanical embodiment or center of that sentient part that is in fact present in the body.

Citing the fact that when you are in love. You do not feel it in your brain first; you feel it in your heart. The Heart has traditionally been thought of as the center of the soul.

There are many unexplained things on this planet.

If the brain is corporeal, and it is a mechanical thing made up of protoplasm, then the mind is the entire nervous system working in tandem with that sentient part of you that we know as spirit to deal with current time events, and process and link them in terms of experiences.

That is how memory works. This sentient Crossing-guard makes choices on how to link input with memories.

An example is the almost pathogenic fear of yellow flying insects. The person who had this condition was able to go back and to find out where this memory came from. Then sat to program it out of his mind to where he knew when saw that genre of insect, to be first alarmed, and then to tell himself that they will not bother you if your do not bother them, to then go on about his business.

He took a fear, and programmed it out of his own mind, and this makes one think about what else this technique would facilitate.

As we went through all of this stuff in our own lives, we discovered some of our upbringing that stands in the way of our ultimate success.

Of course, we are talking about those little helpful comments that come to us as children from adults.

So! What is happiness? You should know from personal experience that you have never been happier than when you are "anxiously engaged in a good cause."

So what is your good cause? I call mine, "The Beebe Research Project."

The focal point is, "How can a person who has hit his or her bottom get back up and find him or herself fulfilled, happy, and successful in ways that they perhaps had not been able to imagine before?" This is what we want to tell you. If you apply these things never mind buying a lottery ticket, you are not going to need it!

When fully optimized, you will laugh at the lottery saying, "Who needs it?" You will know that your success is indeed coming soon.

We quote a very noble fellow when we say, "We can see what I see because we stand on the shoulders of giants." We want to give you that information, and say, "Climb on up here, the view is most excellent."

That is what you need when you hit your bottom. You know it. To pretend otherwise is like that great line from Fight Club, "Sticking feathers up your butt does not make you a chicken."

There are the blessed few who never have to make that journey, and then there are the rest of us who are not going to do anything until we hit that point where it is either a choice between slowly dying and doing what you have to in order to make life better for ourselves.

The personal bottom is where if you do not take care of yourself, all that is you will cease to be, your soul dies, and all that is left is an empty shell until the day that you die. That is the point where you have a choice. You have to matter to yourself, and if you do not take care of yourself, and eventually there will be nothing of you left to give to anyone, and you will cease to be as a self-affecting soul.

Eventually you will see that there has to be some sort of a magnificent change made to your life. The question was then what should one do in the meantime?

Many of us are fans of home based business, and the teachings of Robert Kyosaki. We long to be working on establishing successful home-based businesses, and growing it to where it is just too big to run out of the home. For us allot of things remain to be seen so far as results, but there are several ways that you can be as sure as possible of the outcomes that you have sat out to achieve, and that is about half of what this book is going to be about.

The first half of this project is a sort of essay regarding how to set yourself up so that you are guiding every step of your life toward those things that you call your dreams. This is the juice of life.

How do you make those things that you desire to have as a part of your reality into a tangible part of your day-to-day life. The thing is, "How do you come to see your life as both happy and fulfilled?"

It is not so much about money as it is about deciding on what you really want, and getting to work in the pursuit of making it happen!

This is your good cause.

You ought to hold as a truism, now that man is at his best when he is anxiously engaged in a good cause. We shall define good cause as that issue above, (what is going to make you happy and fulfilled in the doing of it).

It is far better to act to make your life better than to the recipient of someone else's action. If you are an effect, an effect there is nothing feeling within you, nothing sentient, mechanical, and almost robotic. We call these people depressed.

It is possible to suppress things so that you cannot act with that sentient part within you, we would suggest that it is something that to avoid. It is, as stated earlier, that sentient feeling is what makes you into you. This part of you wants everything to be at its best.

You ought to be in the sentient awareness and emotion that really makes you want everything to turn out for the best for everyone, including yourself.

There are some insights that came to us. We knew which the right approach was. The approach was that you had to stop worrying about what you cannot do, and define what you can do.

You take that list of things that you can do. Then you pick one in which the doing of it would make you happy. The term for this is finding your passion.

What makes you the happiest?

That is the question. "What of the list of things that you could still do would make me the happiest in the doing of it, and how do you get from where you are to where you really desire to be?"

This is the beginning of progress for all people. The first realization is that you do not have to accept what is just because it is.

You can change many things, but that change has to begin in you.

There is a great deal of truth to the old adage that "It is all in how you look at it!", or, "Attitude is altitude."

In the very same reality, one person might see a failure, while the other might see an opportunity. Now who is going to make a success in this reality?

One would lean toward it being the person who saw the opportunity and chose to act upon it. Recessions are sometimes not accidents. It is like a day at Wall Mart for the truly wealthy. Have you noticed all of the companies recently that have purchased other companies lately?

It was more than luck. They were able to see an opportunity, and able to act upon it.

They were open to it, and prepared to receive it. People who are prepared to see those many opportunities ahead, and prepared to receive them, will change their realities, and have the goals that we all know that they have.

This book is about preparing your mind to have your brain constantly seeking the things that will move you toward your goal. It is also about preparing your soul to do right with the blessings that are coming.

This is the holistic approach to success and power in the right way. It is either a blessing or a test, and that is dependent upon you. Maybe your goals do not involve money, and that puts you in a decided minority.

It is immaterial what your goals are; this will help you to realize them. Now, we would prefer that your goals are honorable.

The rule that your freedom to swing your fist ends where my nose begins, fully applies here and if you hit my nose, you have an enemy.

It works all over the world that way. In every culture, that one is true, and it is true wherever you may happen to be.

If you ignore the spiritual side of this process, you are missing what amounts to the majority of the point of the thing. It is not holistic unless you are working with body mind and spirit to prepare the whole to accept the fullness of the goal. You need to be ready to accept it.

Every change has consequences, and these will change your life. How do you know what the consequences will be? If you do your due diligence in the making your plan phase, you will know what is coming your way and have time to prepare for it.

There is not a great deal of room for surprises in planning your future, and we believe there should never be.

We will go over how to consider your passion, and to align it with what you can do. We will go over the honest self-appraisal process, and planning, as well as goal setting.

We are going to look at the mid course correction, Staying on course, and what to do to keep true to your primary starting point for you in this effort. Now if you think that you are not worthy of success, or that you do not deserve it, there is no way that you will overcome that because you will find that your mind will be looking for ways to sabotage whatever you are trying to accomplish.

We were able to work all that out through NAC (neuro-associative conditioning), and that was by taking the time to identify why one felt so badly about himself, line upon line and precept upon precept, and removing every negative line and precept replacing it with something positive and enabling. This term" neuro-associative conditioning" is literally making a new mental habit after trashing the old one.

This took quite a bit of time, and every moment was worth it. This correction took the better part of nine months, but when it was over it was almost like there was a new man. He had lightning bolts coming out of his backside, and was supercharged.

You are just running around expending allot of energy, and hoping that something works. This is like having a nuclear missile with no guidance system. It packs allot of power, but its purpose is undefined.

Then we had to consider how to focus this thing to the goals that a person had set for the starting point of his endeavors.

What is starting point in your endeavors? Every journey must have both a true beginning and a true end. The end is the glory part, but having a true beginning means that you have been heading in the right direction from the very start.

You need to look at what you propose to do, and understand precisely where you are in terms of that goal. That gives you a good idea of the work that lies ahead.

Now, there are those who think that work is a dirty word. We would echo the Mormon chestnut, which is "Without work NOTHING is accomplished." You know then that you are going to have to put some effort into it.

Therefore, you are better off if you put some effort into something that you enjoy.

This is not a radical thought. Every mogul that we have talked to, or heard interviewed has told the very same story, and that one thing is that you should find your passion, become excellent at it, and the money will find you.

Consider the team of Ben and Jerry. We say that you were at least a couple of bricks shy of a full load if you were to say that they were not passionate about ice cream.

So, how do you combine all of this? It has been a challenge, and it took quite a few changes to figure out how to include multiple basic passions into one plan.

It helps if you are a creative person. It is our contention that the information is out there, such that anyone can get up, and make their life into something beautiful.

Only one can make beauty from ashes. Put credit where the credit is due.

We are going to tell you what we did in this regard because if our study subject can do it with several different passions, you can do it with one or more.

There are several disciplines that you need and GLORY BE! if you should already have them.

He did not and had to learn each one in turn. There is always a learning curve. It is simply true that his was a bit steeper than most.

We can look back on it and chuckle now, but at the point in time when we were looking at this up close and personally, it was serious business.

If an approach fails, try another one but do not give up, and your efforts might just change the world. One thing is for sure, and that is that they will certainly change your world.

The second one is time management. If you have a task to do, you need to get to it and do it. One precursor is that you have knowledge of what to do (at this time) we are assuming that you have done your due diligence, and role modeled).

If that is the case, then if your role model has faced this same issue then you should do what he did, or approximate it as closely as you can within your current legal environment.

You do not want to waste time when you are on task to achieve your goals. Rely heavily on your day planner. If it does not make it to the schedule book during work time, odds are that it is not going to happen, and busy people have every working day planned down to fifteen-minute intervals.

The third issue is one of being a professional in what you are doing. There are times when it is important to look like a professional, but there are no times during your work that it is not important to be one.

Your income is your bread and butter, but your plan is your future, and punctuality tells the person that the reason for your appointment is important to you, and they will approach you in kind.

If you modern normal, spend a good amount of time on the computer, you want to look like a pro when you have "face time," or when you are on a web conference.

When a client can see you, it is very important to look the part, and that is because you never do get a second chance to make a first impression.

A very big part of this equation is product knowledge. There is no excuse for you not to know your product (even if your product is you), be it a good or a service. You need to make it your personal business to become well versed in whatever it is that you do. You are the expert.

All of this plays into something that you can later take to the bank, your reputation. It is your good name. Believe me, business people talk to each other. Having a great reputation is the best thing that you can give yourself in any effort.

Now we come to the aspect of frugality. Wise management of your resources means that you are ensuring your continued survival as a business entity, or any other type of entity as well.

Honest with yourself may just answer that question for you, and that is why we stress the honest self-appraisal. It enables you to know what you have, and what you need to get to make it all happen.

Then it is simply a matter of planning your work and of working your plan. So get to work and make those dreams happen.

The passion part of this makes it all much more enjoyable. Have you ever met anyone who really loved his or her work? We do.

The goal of this text is to teach you how, on all of the relevant levels to make certain that the goals that you have chosen are the right ones for you.

You train your mind in how to seek out those opportunities to make those objectives come to life such that you are on your way to achieve and be happy. In whatever it is that you propose to do you need to know what success feels like.

You are not successful until you feel successful, and how you rise above a defeatist attitude is to wake up every day and say," I'm successful, although I have yet to convince my banker of it." Then you know for that day what you must do in order to convince my others of it.

You might want to stretch this work out into a five year plan, and I have done what I suggest for you to do, and that is to take the work and divide it over your time period for your goal so that you know what you must do every single day to make those goals happen over time.

If you will only get to that point, and do those daily tasks religiously (faithfully and without exception), you will be drawn to your goals as easily as breathing, and as naturally.

It is very true that when you approach your goals, it is all in how you look at it. If you deal with it as a professional, you will find that you will get professional results, and they will astound you.

There is something to wonderful about feeling astounded at the level of your own success. There is nothing like looking at your results and being speechless, except for the word, Wow!"

Be proud. Every goal that you have will come your way, so long as you can manage the workload.

One of the criteria for additional goals is that they must not require a great commitment of time. You might want to keep some time for those things that you really enjoy. That is the juice of life. To be able to do them without worry is wonderful.

SRB

Chapter One

DIGGING OUT FROM UNDER THE RUBBLE

Some of the largest blocks to realizing our best results come from the helpful notations that come from well intentioned people in our youth and childhood. Yet there are many other things at play here.

You might face issues of poor self-image or a lack of faith in yourselves. There are spiritual, psychological, and emotional issues that may come before and interfere with your progress toward what is going to make you happy.

One would be derelict in naming this chapter "Digging out From Under the Rubble" without being very specific about what that rubble Is, and then telling how to deal with these things in kind.

There is not one person who is aware of world events that would not say that our world has problems.

The Christian idea or understanding of these problems is that we live in a world that created to be a paradise, when people began to choose wrong over right in the world; the world entered a fallen state.

If it were not in a fallen state, then bad things would never happen to good people, and this would be a globe of perfect justice.

The sad truth of it is that some people do not seek justice but advantage over others.

If the Earth was completely in a purely fallen state, this would always be true, and yet here I am to tell you that you can be successful and happy and never cheat anyone.

We do live in a fallen world, but that does not mean that we must all be fallen creatures. We can strive for things that are higher and nobler, and we can do so without guilt or regret.

To be able to know that this was indeed true became a goal. We had to see a successful enterprise that founded on doing good, and the win/win scenario was the order of the day.

Now there are people that espouse the win/win, and they are doing it as lip service to a concept, but we are talking about a corporation in which their representatives earn because the condition of their clients is better for having dealt with them. If you do not better the state of your client, and then you do not gain. Wow! what a concept.

Some network and other companies operate on this premise, but the first one that caught my attention was an insurance company.

They taught their agents courses in listening to the client's needs, desires, and take notes.

There are others. Again, the world is in a fallen state, but we can rise above it for ourselves by how we handle our business as well as the business of our lives.

You should not make things worse by choosing to do wrong. People abdicate this god-given responsibility on a daily basis because it is often easier to, or more convenient.

We use terms like white lie, and necessary evil. Is that "evil" really necessary, or is it just the easy way out?

Can you run a business, and do the right thing as a matter of habit? Can you do the right thing even when there is an option that costs less?

You know that in the end that will flow back to you in terms of reputation and that intangible asset that can be worth millions, "GOODWILL."

One of the big problems with business is that we tend to see tomorrow as long term planning.

Yet it is true that goodwill today is money in the bank tomorrow. Then we can look at how we live our lives, if it is something that we find interesting.

In short, quoting Stephen King who wrote something on the order of," Ghosts are real, spooks are real, and demons are real. They live within us, and sometimes they win."

These things based in experience, and sometimes they based in experience that nobody could have seen coming.

This is the very strongest argument for past lives. Take for example the serial killers that have come from good homes, and based on some programming that they did not get from their home life; they go out and start taking lives at will.

We are not implying that you should believe in past lives, but one must have cause to wonder where those mental links, for example that turn a brilliant mathematician into a "Unabomber" who simply blows away the competition. They have to come from somewhere. Mental snaps do not just happen. We create them over time. So what I am saying is that something happened to cause the break

These demons appear to link at some time in childhood, and they just sit there like dormant bombs waiting for the next piece of the trigger to fall into place. It seems that there are so many variables in the human brain that there cannot be one specific seed, but they are specific to the individual brain.

Then with the individual brain, they link in unique ways, and in the innocence of youth, we make our oath that these things are true.

They may not be.

The very best way to avoid that hazardous oath is to take control of the helm of your own ship, so to speak. One of the major causes of this downward spiral is the continued feeling of hopelessness, and we want to tell you, and convince you that there is hope, and you can take control of your life, and break through the barriers between you and your ultimate fulfillment and happiness.

We look at all of the people that fit into the above classifications that we have studied in the beginning of this venture, and all one can say is, "There but by the grace of God go I".

How is it that someone who is going down in a world of swirl can get a do over in life? "World of swirl" is a Texas expression meaning the condition in the bowl after the flush.

Still, that is a very good question. We plan to try to be succinct in the answer, but it so powerful that brevity would surprise you.

When we were children, certain events taught us that we had to try to make the best of the hand that dealt to us, and that made many of us feel hopeless, and powerless.

Now; this is going to sting a bit, but it works. No matter what has happened to you, you have to take ownership of the event. We do not distinguish between a pristine Norman Rockwell sort of childhood, and the person who endured the most vile forms of abuse, you have to take ownership of it or you cannot change it. This is not to say that it was or was not your fault, but only that you have to accept in your mind that it happened, and deal with it, and eventually forgive the perpetrator or forgive yourself.

You may fight against the slide into mediocrity, but you wind up doing things that amount to self sabotage.

It is very curious as to what, on an intellectual level what is wrong, when one cannot seem to put it together and make it work.

That was because we were starting at the now, when we needed to look back and assess whatever it was that was making our subject think that he did not deserve to happily achieve.

For him, it was not about the money, but about proving that he could do it.

We went into this knowing that if we could successfully bring one of his goals to fruition that he would have a taste of success.

At one time during this work our subject was judged to be worthy of a Social Security Disability. This gave us what we needed, an amount of time to think.

As the clouds began to clear, the idea or realization came to us that it is not all, about what he cannot do, but rather about what he can do.

Now, there is something very powerful about writing it down. We then had the thought to make a list of all of the things that he knew that he could still do.

Then the wheels began to roll. We had a rather large list, and we understood that we had to cut it down to only one choice. This would get our subject started toward re-discovering his life.

The age-old debate between heredity and environment shows up right here. There were things that he liked because he grew up doing them with his adoptive family, and there were other things that he liked to do that seemed to have no source or reason, and there was no explanation for the propensity in his visible family.

When we got deeper, he had passion for things on both sides of this spectrum.

We learned a great deal, but lacking a proper state of mind, he could never put it together and make it work. There was still something missing.

None of these are completely Incompatible, and if planned out well enough. We knew that he could eventually have all of them, at least on an intellectual level. There was all of that programming that had to be removed, and so it became a task of ferreting out these things, and dealing with them in a way that would help him to both organize his life, and to remove all of those negatives that were roadblocks to his success.

This is where we get technical. We knew neuro-associative conditioning from experience, and that was the first stop. When we identified a problem we then attacked it, and all of them worked, would say things to the subject specifically tailored to discredit the linkage, and then would then input something new and positive, and empowering.

If replacing linkages does not do the trick as you go through the process, you may need to apply stronger techniques, or do it again.

You are not in error to have a mistrust of the "psycho-pharmacological" industry, and therefore we cannot recommend them in good conscience.

There was one measure between neuro-associative conditioning, and psychological treatment, and that is something that we are reluctant to push. If push came to shove, the next step after this is therapy, and that is costly, and not immediately effective.

You are very well able, in most circumstances to be your own therapist using this technique. If you are honest with yourself then the question is, "Who knows more about you than you?"

Our subject craved order, and any person who has his personal house in order has realized that you should order yourself first, and then take the time to order your environment briefly.

You are an individual, and you are observant enough to know when your environment is in order.

It took him a while to get to that point, but doggone it he finally got there. Ordering your personal house is another story indeed.

This is something that you have to rely on your intuitive nature to figure out. The truth of the matter is that if you feel that something in your nature is incongruent with your vision of what you desire in your life, then it most likely is incongruent, and therefore a change is in order.

Of course, the first step to making a change is realizing that there is a problem, and then you have to make the decision to change whatever it is into something that is both congruent, and supportive of your goals.

We would reiterate the process of neuro-associative conditioning for you, but it is above, and you can refer back to it, if you need to. If 75 cycles of this does not do it, I suggest repeating the process, and then consider stronger measures.

We have all experienced many kinds and manner of pain in our lives, and then as nature abhors a vacuum, It is necessary to come up with an appropriate counter-statement that was empowering, and supportive of one's goals. It takes a little thinking.

The very basic human decision-making process is a process of pleasure and pain.

We will intuitively seek things that we believe will give us pleasure, and we will do almost anything to avoid pain.

The exception is senseless acts of self-sacrifice. It is like throwing yourself on a live grenade to save the other people in your squad. That is the proverbial horse of another color.

Nobody is asking you to sacrifice your life for the greater good here. It is basic to the premise that you associate the bad linkage with a tremendous amount of pain, and associate the new alternative with as great of a source of pleasure as possible.

If you can get your brain to accept this, you can change almost any bad linkage in your mind, and thereby redirect your life toward your goals.

For the very few issues that are exceptions, you have a hierarchy of alternatives. There are three.

The first alternative is to give up, and nobody wants to do that, Giving up on your dreams is the coward's way out, but if you just keep on trying to make those changes in approach, I would recommend prayer with stronger therapies.

This just seems to energize things and move them along much quicker. It helps to believe and acknowledge a higher power.

There is nothing wrong with moving things along. In psychological growth, either you are growing or you are dying, and there is not any third direction. You, clearly, will want to keep up a consistent growth in this matter. If you are facilitating the success in your mind, you are progressing toward these goals, and in the direction that you want.

Now, just because you have some issues over the long run is no reason not to get started on this goal seeking work of yours in tangible ways.

When hurdles arise, you deal with them, rise above them, and move on. That is why I called my business, Marathon Research. It is because I am in it for the long run, and before the end of 2010, I had it organized.

Do you remember when we spoke about being frugal? The rule of thumb is that you have to start somewhere, and just work from there.

You really do not have to worry so much about survival. The real issue is getting the best use out of what you have right now.

FROM THE SUBJECT

"Then came October and November of 2009, and that was the time when my "national anthem" may well have been George Clinton's "Tear The Roof Off that Sucker". I decided to look into Graduate school, into the Masters of Business Administration Program Online.

I was in Portland, Oregon, and that was the best online Masters that I found in my field and Portland did not have one in Supply Chain Management, and so I climbed aboard for the ride, and used a part of the surplus to facilitate an upgrade in technology, and fund the home based business startup."

This man was on a Social Security Disability, and now he is gainfully self-employed, and loving his life.

"By the end of the year, I was on my way up, with no turn around in sight. I got a Mulligan in life folks, and it was not a matter of luck. It was a matter of finally making some decisions and acting upon them."

It blinded us with science! This stuff worked so wonderfully well that I was thinking about fulfillment of all of our own goals, and planning strategies to make them incredible.

I sat a goal of learning something new every day and making a new discovery. That gives your brain anticipation, and helps people to awaken joyously in the morning and be ready to face another day.

If it is all in how you look at it, this is a definite advantage. Many people never, and I mean all the way back into childhood, never wake up perky.

Now I am excited to meet the new day, and meet the challenges of it. How did I turn it around?

I think that I have already told you. Persistence in the processes proved to work from the beginning.

There is a somewhat cliché saying," If it works, don't fix it." That just makes sense, but it is important to maintain the things that do work.

We want you to have firm legs to stand on as you reach for your own stars. You need to turn things that work for you into productive habits.

The psychology behind all of this is that you need to go forward. If something moves you forward, you need to go with it, so long as the direction it is pointing you in is the direction of your goals.

If it is not, and at a point of evaluation, you feel that this direction is not congruent with you goals, you need to consider making some changes.

The business cycle does not allow you, if you are working this thing correctly to move without correcting your course. It allows you to correct your effort's course many times before you get to the end zone and make that big score. This is a great blessing and a wonderful tool for those who, like me would happily achieve.

You would think it is amazing how things all come together to help you when you look at them in the proper fashion? Do you really think that is an accident?

You will find many things like that, which will aid you in the passionate pursuit of your dreams. One can say that because there is a level of joy in the seeking of it that it makes your work almost like play.

Now as our subject got into graduate school I found myself getting hugely busy because he also sat up his home based business around the same time, the workload was amazing, and he enjoyed every minute of it. He was working about 45 hours a week. This gave him about an hour a day for the gym, and an allotment of about three hours a week for a social life, and two hours for church.

You have to know that with all of this work, he should soon see everything that he ever wanted in his life as a reality it is a sort of a natural law. Effort always brings results, and it is focusing the effort on the things that you really want that makes life and the pursuit of these things a joyous experience.

We all have known these things since childhood, and yet, when we saw it happen before our eyes, it came as a bit of a shock.

Intellectually, we always knew that it was possible, but never imagined that we would be able to feel like that about ourselves. We all are now happy and achieving. We are now happily achieving.

I have chosen my passion, and you must choose your own simply because that passion you choose is your own. Your passion is a very personal thing.

What is it that you desire to do the most? What would be your best life and what are you doing in it. This answer has to be honest, and it should not be, "I want to be rich."

That is just lame, because the things that we want are possible having money, Money is a means and not an end. If money is an end for you, change your priorities or you will die old rich and alone.

Nobody is comforted at that time in life if he or she is alone. It is also true, and as much as I do not like quoting any Church leaders in my writing, it is very true that "No success in this world can compensate for failure in the home."

So; to begin this process, you have to have a clear idea of the material things you want in your reality, and the types of things that you would want to be doing in that reality.

Catch a vision.

King Solomon, perhaps the most wise man that ever walked the earth said, "Without a vision the people perish." This is true, and it works on every sociological level that you can envision. The first step in happily achieving is to have a vision of your best life. So what is the nature of your best life?

There is always time to get to work for your future. In your zeal never forget that you have a family because it. I believe was a fellow named Norman Mclean who wrote," It is those that we love, live with and know that elude us".

If you are a family man or woman, these are your first priority, your family. Many wish that they had known what we are sharing with you in their twenties because if they had, their families would have had a much better life. Sorrow and a dollar can get you a cup of coffee, unless you hit a point where you can insure that you will not cause or carry any further sorrow intentionally for the remainder of your life.

We learned that if you give and you do not take care of yourself appropriately, soon enough, you are not going to have anything else left to give.

"Mens sano en corpore sanum," (A Healthy mind in a healthy body) was the marching orders of the Roman army, and as you take care of your body better, you will find that the clarity and the power of your mind increases as well. A healthy mind in a healthy body is true indeed.

You do not need coffee, or energy drinks, just do that you will be able to rock and roll all day long.

What makes you want to turn it around? Do you remember where we discussed the pleasure and pain basis of basic decision-making? The simple truth of the matter was that you get to a point that the pain of going through your life, the way that it had become, that the idea of waking up in the morning was met by a loud scream of "NO!!!!"

The idea of more of the same becomes intolerable. There has to be a change, and the question of whether or not to change was moot.

You have to change, but the question of the day is "How and in what direction?"

You then have sought guidance and have started to pray. Ii is not so much that you believed that it would help, but you felt and also knew that it could not hurt, and then lacking any expertise, you listened to the feelings that came your way about that change.

It is necessary to be quite firm when we tell you that some of those feelings were things that you will know could not come from you. They will be just too wise, and at the time, the most generous of souls would never have referred to most of us as wise.

These feelings came from outside of you. You have to attribute that to your higher power.

In the serenity prayer, we ask for" the serenity to accept the things that I cannot change, to change the things that I can change, and the wisdom to know the difference."

We cannot, in good conscience advocate divorce, but marriage is, after all one of the primary causes of divorce. If you can fix it, then fix it. If not, then all I can say is that it may be better to end it than to remain miserable, and let it interfere with your future.

Your partner should make you a better person, and vice-versa, and if that is not the case, then you have a decision to make. If that partner is tearing You down, and not building you up, the two of you need to have a long talk and see if the relationship has run its course.

If the two shall be as one, then if that partner is tearing you down, then there is something wrong in him or her that needs fixing, and if they are unwilling to fix it, then run, and do not look back.

That was one of the things that you can do, stop looking back! You cannot change that past, and to try to is ever so very much foolishness. You can only have so much foolishness until you are a fool.

You would prefer to people see you as a successful person.

Then if you had sat down in writing, what you are passionate about, in terms of your life, and the realities that you would like to see in your day-today world.

You can combine this knowledge, to answer the question of where to start.

I would suggest that you start with something that is going to give you little tastes of success on a regular basis. Once you experience them, your brain is going to want more.

That would give you an order of task-oriented success every day, and I must admit that when you really taste of success, the brain just craves for more. There was wisdom in that choice, and it was not my wisdom.

They say nobody ever gains wealth until they become in control of their taxes. Then the way to gain control of your taxes is to make your entire life tax deductible, and that is something that you can do with the help of a good accountant or a competent tax attorney, or even with yourself having a thorough notion of how the tax system works.

An example of this would be the fact that I made my housing, utilities, vehicles, fuel, and even a food budget a corporate expense, under the corporate by-laws, and therefore my salary is a separate matter. Initially, I did not give myself very generous of a salary because the business was paying for everything, almost.

A good idea is to install the self-tithe concept. If you can work it into your budget, and meet your needs (not wants), you would channel ten percent of your gross income into a capital savings account.

This provides you with resources and incentive to make the building up of income producing assets to a point where your money is working for you, and the harder that you money works for you, the less you have to. This places you in control of your money and not having your money in charge of you.

The point is that you finally had to take control and responsibility for where you are, and had to take control of your destiny.

Nobody ever taught us how to do that, and as we looked at it, that would have been a marvelous preparation for adult life, but instead we just had to figure it out at some point in our lives.

You have to become passionate about finding your answers. If you need those answers badly, then we suggest that you make it a personal research project, and get those answers for yourself so that you can have the basis of your new life, the life that you desire the most.

We are going to get into conquering the contra-indicators of the possibility, even the street savvy, which we all lacked at one time or another.

They say that I Q increases with age, but I cannot vouch for that because I have done some very stupid things between my youth and now, and this quip toward by me dad at a moment of frustration with me. He said, "You have to be smart to act stupid because if you are stupid, man you're just not acting."

During some of my escapades as a somewhat errant youth, he was frustrated, and said, "Son; I know that you are smart, you thought this stuff up, and no dummy could pull it off, but you did, and God help me, I do not know how".

I did not want to be a skilled artisan. I did not know what I wanted to be. I knew some things that I wanted and enjoyed, but I had in no way settled on what I wanted to do when I was grown up.

I am not what one might call handy. It is just not me. I am a "call the guy" kind of a man; I am no good at things that involve home maintenance. They are not a part of my environment. My interest is in business. My interests, which expand to writing, education, and performing arts, all come from the gene pool, and the intelligence which somehow remains intact has allowed me to make a plan to work my life so that I can actually do all five of these things, just not at the very same time. If I enjoy this set of five activities the most, then I should have some aspect of all of them in my life to maximize my self-concept of success, and if I should not try to work in all of them, I would never know which is going to be my best path. I am open to the eventually of winnowing it down to one activity, but I love all five and am passionate about each of them.

At worst, I would have to give up four of them, but at least I would have known that I gave the failing four my best shot, and I can live with that.

If you have made a decision and have your passion(s) defined, and have a basic plan, but that is not and never will be good enough for a long term goal. For this game, you need a thorough long-term plan. So, how do you put that plan together?

Chapter Two

ROLE MODELING AND YOUR PLAN

We cannot stress the importance of the idea that success leaves trails, and you are best served when you follow them.

So as often as you can, you should study the people who have done what you really want to do, and then you chose one, and created for yourself behavioral profile. Then you follow what they have done. Then you will have the fun task of creating a plan to make it to where you would have the ability to take a shot at all of these things within the shortest period possible.

At this point in the story is where the real work begins. The level of tiredness that you feel when you are trying to make your best life is a good tired. Maybe you used to have trouble sleeping, but when this is your state, you will sleep like a rock.

The first thing necessary to overcome any of these glitches is to know and to remember and to believe with all of your heart that you are the master of your own destiny.

This is not conjecture, but a natural law of sorts. You, and nobody else is responsible for where you are today, and you are responsible for the ultimate outcomes of your life. Nobody is going to do it for you.

The world will do its best in order to convince you that someone else is responsible, and has the right to control your outcomes. They only have that right if you give it to them. That is the very basis of Government by the consent of the governed. It is natural and the right way to do things.

If you are a follower, be very careful whom it is that you follow. Make sure first that their goals are, at the very least congruent with your own.

In order to be effective you must have immense determination because you care very deeply about the outcome.

What we are trying to accomplish is very simply to show you the very best and smartest way to create the life that you have always wanted.

Of course, it is somewhat more difficult than following the path of least resistance, but mediocrity is not what you want here.

You want to become excellent at whatever it is about which you are passionate.

This world is big enough that whatever it is that you are passionate about, if you are excellent at it, the money will find you. As we look at this, we are starting to find out just how true this is.

You might say, this is very simplistic, and very altruistic, but for those of us who are making the journey, it is fact.

Someone once said, "Whether you believe that you can, or whether you believe that you can't, you're right." I would only ask that you keep an open mind and imagine with us as we go through the rest of the program, and you will see that what we are telling you is fact.

If you are in it to win it, the one thing that is going to be the biggest help is to have the best plan possible for you. The whole point of this chapter is to clue you in on the very best and most reliable ways for you to make a plan that is going to draw you to your goals as naturally as breathing.

The idea here is to make things so very easy that you do not really have to think about them. The plan, when cut down into things that you have to every day to make your goals happen on schedule, so you don't think about those things, or stress over them, you just do them.

Having a clear and precise plan makes goal seeking ten times easier than it would be flying by the seat of the pants. For all that, the bravado is worth, somebody succeeds when flying by the seat of his pants at a real rate of roughly thirteen percent of people who have a precise plan.

The swashbuckling captain of my own ship thing is so romantic. The point is that while 90% of those who do it with a well thought out plan will succeed, while 11.7% of those who just take off down the path will succeed.

The dramatic improvement in the statistical probabilities is something to think about, as you can have a much narrower field to decide from, and the task is then to pick the one that you would desire to do the most, and start working from that point

How do you make your plan such that you maximize its probability of successful completion?

There really is only one way that we know of, and the first thing is to know the processes of what you are dealing with. If for example, you are making ice cream, you will want to have a good knowledge of how to do that. First, you want to have a clear definition of success in your mind, then you want to study someone who has succeeded (for example) at the commercial making of ice cream, and then you simply need to know how he or she did it, and do what he or she did.

This is the role modeling process. It will show each condition of success in the goal that you seek, and where you are in terms of the goal right now.

Then the plan is simply to mark the pathway between both points. If you look at the chart, you can then take the conditions of success, aspect by aspect, and know what you have to do to get from point A to Point Z (the end of the journey). You know the full extent of the work. So what do you do with that information?

Do you recall the old chestnut," How do you eat an elephant? "The answer is one bit at a time.

Likewise, you break the work down into bits of a manageable size. You do this by merely dividing it over the expected duration until you have the goal as a part of your everyday reality.

If you expect a time span of five years until you will be able to realize the goal, then you would break it down into an annual goal, arbitrarily by dividing the work by five. Quarterly goals are done by dividing by four, and then into monthly goals by dividing by three. Weekly goals arise by taking the accounting 4.3 weeks per month. The final step is to divide that by however many days you will work in a week to get your daily goals, and if you do that daily work every working day, you are going to find that you are drawing toward your goals. It is like a karmic magnet.

You are putting the proper work into the process, and the proper results will happen. Then you will have the satisfaction of knowing that you are making wonderful things happen in your life. The marching orders are, "IF IT IS TO BE, IT IS UP TO ME."

The plan shows you the way. Now when you are looking at where you have come in a given period of time, and you see that you are somewhere short of the mark, you have to make a decision on what to do in order to get your goal back on course. If you happen to be above where your estimations showed that you should be for the moment, there would be nothing wrong with simply letting it roll, and perhaps being above your final goal.

If that is the case, then you shift the next period up accordingly and keep on going. If you see that, you are under your goal this is what we call the "midcourse correction.

This is not a quick fix. It is going to involve a doubling, and perhaps a redoubling of your efforts over the next period in order to get back on track, or perhaps it is something that you can do with one quick change.

The call is yours because the expertise is yours. Make the call.

Sometimes if intelligence does not point, you in that way and until other things are resolved, and you find a spiritual peace, these great truths rarely avail themselves to you. Why?

The truth of the matter is that we sometimes are living in darkness of our own design. We fail to see what was truly real about ourselves and about others. This may be why we marry so very badly sometimes.

Perhaps you could not see the truth about her either. (Lucky are the people who marry well)

After my divorce, I used to pray for the clouds to fall away so that I could see the whys and wherefores of my own life, and in every sense of the words, to take responsibility for my past, and under my God to take responsibility for my future.

We hold the theory that a passion is a calling. We think that the creator to move you to what you were meant to do put it there. Some say that "if you have a desire, then you should do the work".

We firmly believe it without hesitation. The result of pursuing your passion is that you will work harder, stronger, and longer because if you are passionate about what you are pursuing. Then the efforts in behalf of that goal are more like play, and less like work to you, and indeed, it is all in how you look at it.

This is where the neuro-associative conditioning comes in. It is part of being self-aware enough to know that there is a problem with your outlook.

If some way that you are thinking is being a roadblock to your success, then you have the tools at hand to help your correction. Sometimes you will find that you need a correction in your thinking to promote a positive change in your path toward your goal. This process will help.

Every mind is unique, but there are certain things that we all have in common.

What you have to do is to create a mental habit. This is how we train the mind to rid itself of the roadblocks of the past, and then you create a new and empowering paradigm, by associating the new positive and empowering belief with the creation of great pleasure. This works like a charm, and the period that it takes depends on how much free time you have to go through it. For me, a cycle of 75 repetitions takes about two and a half hours (total time over a few days).

Then, based on the advice of a former Miss America, I just, "Fake it till I make it." I act as though the new paradigm is in place, until it really is in place and working.

On occasion you will run up against a way of thinking that neuro-associative conditioning cannot change, Repeat cycle, and then get stronger helps in place. Sometimes, you just need to show your brain that the old thought paradigm is in error.

An example of this might be my former belief in what I called French Revolution Theology. I had to find a business that was successful, and was not cheating anyone.

When I found one, my aversion to making myself successful changed very quickly. I had seen firsthand. My belief was in error, and the brain simply took care of business.

Proper conclusions will avail themselves down the road. The plan remains your roadmap to your future, and regardless of what mental things that happen, you pledged to do whatever the plan directs. In the face of new information, you can modify or alter parts of the plan, as you need to. It is your plan, and within reason, and without changing the goal, you can do whatever you want to with it. The orientation of that change should be to enhance your shot at making your goal.

If it impedes your goal, you are derelict as a goal seeker if you choose contrary options. It is all eyes on the goal, my friends, and if you ever take them off, you are not going to get there.

We are most decidedly against radically making changes in the plan, but sometimes they are necessary, and expedient. One example might be that when you are about to engage in a project, and you find that a part of it is now illegal, then you have to work around that particular issue and that you really need to be precise.

You begin with that very honest self-appraisal looking at every aspect of the goal that you propose to seek, and not exactly, where you are in terms of that aspect of the goal. This requires a level of candor that we very seldom allow ourselves. The necessity of the candor is one of pure logic. If you are aware of your current circumstances, it allows you in a very clear way to see what it is that you need before you attain that goal that you seek. You have to ask yourself with the greatest candor, "How long under current reality is it going to take me to accomplish this goal?"

Remember that a goal without a time frame attached to it is merely a dream, and we all have dreams, but who turns those dreams into a tangible part of their daily reality?

We find that a mentor really helps, and in the absence of a mentor, the role modeling approach works wonders.

It is a great blessing if you actually have a friend that has done what you choose to do because a mentor is up close and personal.

This is someone who can literally take you by the hand and teach you everything.

There are going to be people who are going to come out of the woodwork, and vehemently oppose your efforts. They are likely your competition.

Then there will be the" nay-Sayers." The nay Sayers are the worst because they hit you on a psychological level and that is where you live. I have to ask, if they are such experts, why are they not doing what you are doing?

Competition is the means that brings excellence. It makes us all better. Without a little competition, businesses get lazy, and they do not improve over time. Competition is healthy, as iron sharpens iron, so competition sharpens business. It is nothing to fear if you are good at what you do.

This is the faith that I have in you. You are not average, you are better than that, or you would not be seeking this sort of advising.

You honestly need to succeed. There is something in you that very strongly desires to excel.

There we have the reason that you are going through all of this stuff. My job is to show you how to maximize yourself for success. It is not easy, but it is very well worth it.

Everybody needs hope, and the belief and knowledge that can make things better. They need to know how to do that, and have confidence that the plan that they have made will succeed.

Here is a very tangible thought. The one thing that will make your success assured is you. We really believe that God wants his people to succeed. Whatever you believe him to be. If he created you, and he placed that passion in your life, then could there possibly be a reason that he would not want you to succeed in it? I do not think so.

We see that no matter how bad it gets, anything is possible. We have seen many people hit their rock bottom, and turn it around.

The only two reasons that are almost uniformly in place are first that their situation caused them sufficient pain to motivate them to do anything they can do to change. Secondly, when things are down, something drives us to turn to deity.

I wonder why when things get good, it is always, "Look what I did." We know that only a fool fails to recognize the hand of God in all things.

If you come across a situation, for the sake of argument, like a general whose armies won the battle, and there is no logical or statistical reason for the win, guess what; God won it for you.

You are then derelict, if you do not thank him for it, and make some correspondingly appropriate public statement.

My job is not to convert you, and I will not try, but it is to show you the way. I hold true to the big blue book of alcoholics anonymous, which says that at your bottom, you need to seek a higher power.

For all intensive purposes, if you pick your doorknob, that is okay. It is a start, and if you are paying attention, on that level, and you are seeking that higher power, I have no hesitation in saying that I know that he will find you.

It is sort of fascinating to say that life is really getting interesting, and every new day is a new adventure, and though the thought is that you now find yourself greeting a new day with a measure of excitement, and the words," Okay what have you got in store for me today?". Then I add, "Well; let's get it done."

Then we impart to ourselves in a day of discovery and growth. There is a wonderful thing that for you. We suggest keeping a journal. It is very simple, and if you record the important things that happened during the day, you can look back on it, and see how you have grown over a period. It also gives you a written record of how your life unfolded. It is a nice thing to look and see how you gave grown and become motivated enough to get up off of your backside and really experience life.

Some would blame anyone and everyone except himself or herself because we did what we thought was right on almost all occasions. This can lead to wondering why you received punishment for things that were not your fault. This is the basis of irrationality. Truth is that some things are your fault and others are not.

We have to realize and take responsibility for the things we have done, and thereby contributed to the train wreck that we see in life.

We suppose that is why confession is good for the soul. Get it out and then you have more space to work with.

Something else begins to happen, and that was very interesting. Our subject began to feel astonishingly better physically; He got a gym membership, and began to get into shape.

If you are going to seek the creator, you need to listen when he makes something known to you.

This is something that really is in your best interest. Never ignore the creator in your efforts. It just does not pay off.

Now what happens if you have your plan says something, and in the course of time, you find that you see that is a bad move on a spiritual level? You should go with the spiritual inclination, and take it on faith.

That is hard for me because I am, while being a confident believer, a bit of a scientist, and an excellent skeptic. I will question everything to the degree that it is going to take me to draw a valid conclusion.

When I have made a valid conclusion, then I stand by it until there is a valid proof that I was in error. Being subject to error is all part of being human.

They say that you cannot control what happens but you can control how you deal with those things. Moreover, so if you react to an obstacle in a positive fashion, and calmly find a way over, under, around, or through that obstacle, that keeps you on target to your goals, then the idea is that you expect positive results.

You will find a certain amount of karma in the process. "That which you sow ye shall also reap."

One does not sow wheat and harvest onions, and likewise one does not sow discord and contention, and reap positive results.

The ideal is that you need to study it out and make an informed decision, and then act to correct the situation. This is the best thing that you can do, and remember that finding help occurs when people see you act at uprightly at times that the going is tough.

Then when people see your mettle, they seem to want to join in and assist, and where help comes from, just might shock you.

People have a habit of falling in behind a winner. The thought that you just might just be a winner may be one that is foreign to you. God knows that it was foreign to me, for the major part of my life.

I just could not conceive of myself being a winner. Sure people said, "That boy's a real winner," but they did not necessarily mean it the same way, but more in the derogatory fashion of the word.

You have to start wherever it is that you have to start. It was mysterious, but I am happy to report it; that when I started writing that in time my mind commanded me to sit down at the PC and type anything and there the truth is.

This is how I became a writer. Before that time, writing was to me, nothing more than cheap psychotherapy, but that cheap psychotherapy left me enough material to do about 29 years worth of books, with a bit of retooling.

Writing something every day is habitual, and that is how you build successful habits.

To find an association that will get behind and promote your work is a blessing indeed.

When it comes, you are on your way. That is all part of the help coming out of the woodwork, but you know that this does happen.

My point is that you find those resources because the mind was actively seeking them. If you have come to believe first that you deserve success, and that there is success out there for me in what you need to do.

Sometimes location is conducive to production, and everybody has a favorite place. As a businessperson, and as someone who specializes in certain business issues, the Houston, Texas area is sort of like Mecca to a follower of Islam. It is the center of my world, and a darned good place to distribute things.

Enough of that stuff. I just wanted to show you that my dreams are happening, and there would seem to be very little that I can do right now to stop it. I was very serious when

I talked about achieving those goals as naturally as breathing. I am able to say that I know it is true because I am doing it.

It is wisdom if you find a group of like-minded people; of people who are happy achievers, and are approximately your age, and report to each other and encourage each other and you would have no concept of just how motivating that is.

Something they call the sigmoid curve. I am going to preach to you a bit, so hang on.

The sigmoid curve is a measure of market penetration in any specific product or class of industry.

We look at the sigmoid curve. There is a level at this curve where the geometry of the thing becomes a geometric upward curve. It is the concept of the product life cycle. If you are getting into a business this is where you need to get into it.

Lifecycles are in a bell curve of various shapes. The economics of it is that if you get into that product or industry just when it is beginning to curve upward, wealth will be yours.

This is what Naisbitt was writing about in his book MEGATRENDS. These days, ignoring a megatrend can be fatal to your efforts.

Therefore, when you consider these things, you want to see where your industry is in terms of the sigmoid curve. Then you catch a wave, and you are sitting on top of the world.

It sounds very simplistic. Yet, these days that is how it is. The worst thing from a financial point of view is to get in near the top and hold on too long.

You see opportunities in terms of the sigmoid curve.

Find your passion, become excellent at it, and the money will find you." There is that thing, the reputation for excellence.

It is challenging when you live in an instant society. Building a reputation for excellence, and getting the word of mouth advertising that it takes, takes a great deal of time. Sometimes it can take years.

Therefore, if you are not getting into one of those megatrends, you need to be persistent and patient, and your goals will happen.

Patience is a virtue. Patience is something that you need in any effort, though it seems hard to come by. It is like in the rearing of children. You must keep working. When they finally get what you have been trying to teach them, what a joyous experience for you. It means that the work was worthwhile after all. It is a validation of all of your effort.

This is why you need to celebrate every achievement every step of the way. Take the time to realize that benchmark, and even reward yourself in some tangible way when it comes.

Such things are in process motivation to make it to the next benchmark moment. We forget this thing sometimes.

It is said," Everyone wants to rule the world." Every person fancies himself someone who directs everyone. I do not, and that is mostly because if we tell the truth, I would rather not have the responsibility.

If anything I view these teachings, as Siddhartha said, something to the order of," These are good teachings, but please do not make anything resembling a religion out of them."

I am an observer and a student. I am a teacher, and a scholar. What I am not is some great light that is here to show the world the right way.

It is the nature of a person in this part of society would accept that a phenomenon is real when they observe it, then it is real. It is like the definition of normal. It is a very and consensus based.

Normal is the consensus among a weighted average of a population. Therefore, nobody is normal, by definition.

If you are normal, you are average in every way.

In my case, normal is something that I never really wanted to be. I always wanted to be positively exceptional in something. I wanted to be the person that enters a room and people begin to whisper, "Wow, it's him." I am not so vain that I would assume myself the voice of God, or some sort of messenger from him, unless at some point in my life the creator actually dispatched me to a task.

I am just a writer, and a teacher. What I have told you in these pages is very simply that your plan is all that you have got outside of yourself that can lead you to your goals.

There are resources, and helps that are available, and these will become apparent to you as you begin to work it out. For starters, it is just you and your plan that you have studied and worked out on how to get from where you are to where you need to be, and that has to be enough room for all of your dreams.

If this is not a miracle, I do not know the definition of the word.

The reason for success is amazingly simple, you really like what you are doing, and those who work with you in whatever fashion will notice that.

However, something more important, the people that you deal with as customers will notice it too. It will give them confidence in your work because you pursue it passionately, and if sales figure into this, you will sell more, and there we have it . . .

NOTHING MOVES UNTIL SOMETHING SELLS.

Chapter Three

PASSION AS YOU HAPPILY ACHIEVE

Therefore, finding your passion and making a plan and working in it, will fatten your bottom line.

It is said that if you are not in business to make money, then you should get out of business, mostly because if you do not business will eventually force you out.

The convention is that an outrageous profit is also consensus based. If everyone charges $3 for a bag of chips, and you charge $4+, then you may be gouging on that one issue.

This is why, if you go to various stores, you will find that their prices, at least in the main line stores, are within ten to twenty-five cents.

Nobody wants to be the bad person and raise prices first, but when one does, they all follow suit.

We see the very same process with gasoline at the retail level. It is important, but that is by no means all that there is to the picture.

If you are positive about buying a new investment property does not mean that owning investment property is going to be a work that makes you happy, and makes your life a never-ending joy, just to be at work.

If you are positive about buying a business, or developing a business, it is not going to make you happy unless that business revolves around doing something about which you are passionate. The point of all of these words is to help you to realize what is going to make you happy, and show you how you can figure out how to make a good living at it.

The passion alone does not determine whether you are going to make money. It determines whether you are going to achieve and be happy with whatever it is that you really want your life to be.

A great part of this is going to be redundant, but if you will remember, how they emphasized things in older texts, by REPITITION. Repetition makes habit.

I regret the redundancy, but it was unavoidable in this case.

First, we are going to start at the surface. Right off of the top of your head, is there something that you feel that you were born to do.

Sometimes people are unable to relocate, that may be for reasons of family, or for other reasons, and that is okay, but. You must address this issue.

If that is the case with you, then you are going to look at things that you can do locally that you would do without pay because it make you happy?

You know your own operative parameters.

Why did I ultimately choose Texas? I am divorced, and my kids are grown. I have no personal linkages that are binding me to Portland, Oregon, and so that left an open door. So, where then optimized that I could achieve all of my goals in one place?

It is my experience and perception, and when it comes down to it, that is about all we have to work with. We have addressed the issues of locale.

You have to deal with the realities that you face, and you have to start wherever it is that you are given geographically and in life.

Sit down and make a list of all of the things that you can reasonably do. This may take you several days because if you are like me, you keep on thinking of things that have not made the list yet.

Then you sit down, when you have determined that this list is in its final version.

We call this the process of elimination approach because now that the list is in its final version, you will cross everything off that you do not know would make you happy in the doing of it. If you do not have a passion for it, it does not make the final cut.

After this, you go to the library, or online, and you find someone who has achieved the one or more things that you are passionate about ad research how they did it.

Know this; if they have succeeded at it, you can too!

Then there are those of us who know exactly that makes us happy in the doing of it. The two times when I was happiest were when my daughter was born, and seeing the look in the eyes of somebody in the audience when I am either talking about something in a teaching format or in performing format when they really get what you are doing.

Both take a great deal of confidence in your abilities. That is why teaching. I think I may have missed my window to be a rock star. Movie star is a one in ten million shot.

As a professor, I can feed the show biz beast in my spare time. I am looking like I can be a professor because I want to, and not because I need the money.

I never thought that I would be able to say that. It all comes from working this process. Finding passion (s) and making a plan, working the plan, and keeping the mind attuned through teaching it to seek out the opportunities to bring the plan to fruition.

There is something tremendous in being able to incorporate the completion of your deepest desires into your daily life by associating of that completion with maximum pleasure, and draw yourself to success.

There are times when intelligence is a roadblock to success. I am familiar with the IQ scores of about twenty very wealthy men, and my IQ is at least twenty-two points higher than the highest of theirs. This is my point, they did not rationalize their way out of doing certain things, but they just knew what they had to do, and that is what they did.

If you have a high IQ, do not allow it to stand in the way of anything. Your mind is a powerful tool and you should respect it as such. You also should be aware that if you see some rationalizing coming up to talk you out of what you know that you need to do, you should get to work with the tools that you have to stop it and re-direct your mind.

Should these things arise, the job is not finished.

Then you have to define the mental habit causing it, go in and "Nac" the heck out of it!

Create a new and empowering mental habit to replace the old one. You just keep fine tuning the process until your brain is like a metal detector on the beach, seeking out opportunities for you to achieve that which you are seeking.

When the job is finished, your mind will keep looking for opportunities to fulfill whatever goal you give it. It is the world's most efficient cybernetic device. Cybernetics is the science of goal seeking.

There is a time when you need ideas nearby. This way, there is no search for them.

You know exactly where it is, and your cybernetic device will find it. Again, here is another point where you are totally in control of your ship.

Gaining a habit of goal seeking is a learning curve. You have decided what it is that you desire to build, and you lay one brick at a time until your dream is a reality.

It is line upon line, precept upon precept, and action upon action. It is very simply this, you desire, you learn, you decide, and you act.

It is every achievement of humankind.

If you have the deep desire to do something positive and productive, this is what we define as a passion. I have to believe that this passion was placed there by the creator, and I am persuaded that it is therefore something that you were created to do.

For those who have no idea what that passion is, I have previously suggested a couple of ways to decide for yourself, but I would suggest that if you have to use them, and you are a praying sort, that you seek to have it spiritually verified, and then you act on it without hesitation.

The thing is that you need to be firmly convinced that the path that you are looking at is the embodiment of the path to your passion.

The answer to that is twofold. First, we have the ability to reason, our minds are curious, and some question everything. The second is free will.

We always have a choice. There would be no justice in the universe, without the natural law that you are always accountable in some way for the results of your choice.

If you make a bad choice, and it winds up hurting your business, well, "Life isn't over yet, get back on the horse, and fix it jack!" If it is to be, it is up to thee!

Never, ever let one mistake keep you from your dreams. It would be tragic. Make one of those wonderful mid-course corrections and get on with it.

To allow one error to stop this process, is giving up, and if you give up, your dreams die.

What follows is the Commencement address that Winston Churchill gave at Harrow in 1941:

> "Never give in. Never give in. Never, never, never, never—in nothing, great or small, large or petty—never give in, except to convictions of honor and good sense. Never yield to force. Never yield to the apparently overwhelming might of the enemy".

This would be our fondest wish for you.

Paraphrasing Shakespeare there are, "No sadder words of tongue or pen than to say what might have been."

Half of the issues surrounding failure arise because people just give up too quickly.

What if Babe Ruth had given up? He still holds the record for most career strikeouts, but he just kept coming to bat because he knew his goal, and that was what he really wanted more than anything did.

He may have been many other things in life, but what he was most focused.

Life is not a quick race. It is a marathon. It is an endurance test, and the only thing that really matters is the condition in which you arrive at the finish line.

There are so many examples of people who simply refused to give up, and they went through a good many bad spells before they got what they were seeking. Finally, they decided to give it one last try, for the 70X7th time, and then they succeeded.

Tenacity accounts for a great deal, but in this text, I have spoken about role modeling. Find someone who has succeeded in the way that you propose to succeed, and do what he or she did. If they made mistakes along the way, well; you might not want to make them too, but if you observe their error, and how they corrected it, then everything that they did to advance their pursuit is simply fair game in your pursuit, except where there might have been a change in the law.

I will tell you that this process will save you scads of trial and error time. If properly applied, this process of role modeling, doing your homework, can save you months, and even years in the pursuit of your goal.

To decide is to make a declarative. This is the way that it is going to be, and no other alternative is acceptable.

If you would do anything less, you are not doing justice to your decision, and that is just sad.

You must be actively focused on your goal and actively seeking it in order to experience the effects of happily achieving. There is nothing like it in the whole world. You can enjoy your work, succeed in mighty ways, and be happy.

People spend most of their lives searching for happiness. Many have gone down to their graves and to their great reward, and have never really tasted of happiness in this life, and I have just disclosed to you where it lies.

Happiness lies in being anxiously engaged in a good cause that you are passionate about. It is in the pursuit!

It does not have to be a business. It can be a charitable cause, or it can be your family, and the rules still ring true; every word of them.

It is true that you can direct your family that you are in charge of in the direction that they should go, but you cannot make them choose it. They have to do that on their own.

There is no better way to help them to choose what is right for them than to be an example, and choose, that which is right for you.

What I am saying is that you I am living proof that you can hit bottom by giving of yourself too much, and not taking time to replenish your own self. One must cultivate one's own garden first.

This is not to say that you should be self-centered, but rather that you need to take care of yourself before you do all of this other stuff.

The Bible tells us that we are to love our neighbors, even as we love ourselves. My retort was always, "But, what if you hate Yourself? . . . the equation would not work then."

It was a true observation, as my later life showed me. One thing that the past several years have taught me is that everyone, individually is important, and must be important for two reasons.

The first reason is the creator made us all, and he does not hold me in any more or less import than Mother Theresa ("For behold, The Lord God is no respecter of persons").

Then the second reason is in order to have a healthy life, you have to take care of yourself because you are the only one who can, or will. Implicit here is a healthy level of self-love.

Have you finally hammered out a plan as to how you will make it happen? You should make yet another decision, and that decision is to work hard and not stop working on this plan until it all comes together, and happens for you, and your life will be flourishing.

When your life is flourishing, you know it, and you will begin to feel happy. This is what I call Happily Achieving, and if you are happily achieving, you know it, and you want to feel it as much as possible.

The struggle to achieve your goals becomes an end unto itself, and you do not need to be encouraged to get to work on it. You are there full force, and you are making it happen because that is what you really desire to do, and you are enjoying every single minute of the process.

How exciting is this?

Now; as you start to feel this excitement, certain things happen within you. Jump headlong into it, and do the work." You will remember a validation for the rest of your life, as your efforts begin to grow exponentially.

There is not a great deal more of prognostication that I can give you in these matters, not knowing what your goals are.

You will know when they appear, and if your excitement and confidence do not grow at that point, I would begin to wonder if you are human.

Then there is the matter of what happens when you wake up one morning, and realize that all of your goals appear.

This is a hard moment for many people because the brain almost inevitably asks, "What's next?"

If you do not have an answer, then there are going to be problems that I call the "Alexander Syndrome."

This may be redundant as well, but Alexander defined himself as a conqueror, and when he saw that there were no more worlds left to conquer, he wept, and then ran upon his sword, killing himself.

We have seen this in recent history with some celebrities, who, when they had achieved their goals, just could not figure out what else to do with their lives. I am certain that you could think of a couple.

There are always new goals out there to achieve. Two words come to mind, expand, and diversify.

Simply take your goal to new heights, or keep that, and get into something different as well.

I love teaching with a new set of goals, and new people to teach, and help, and there are rewards, especially when you help someone to understand the ideas, and processes that you are showing them. There is nothing like the look in the eyes of someone that you are teaching, when they finally get it.

Ongoing rewards and new mountains to climb every term are the things that a teacher finds before him.

We know that life is not a race. The only thing that matters is the finish line. When you get there is when you get there.

We also know that you have a set of talents and abilities at your birth, and we believe that if you do not try to develop those talents, there is accountability for not having done so (though we do not know the nature of that accountability).

Once I realized that this works. I feigned a positive attitude, and everything that I was doing failed. Here is why. I really was not positive.

In this text, we have told you everything about how to become positive. It is a cumulative thing. If you take baby steps of success, and accept the success with each step, eventually you will like that feeling, and you will want it very deeply within your soul. You will seek it, and this makes you positive as a side effect of having tasted of success.

You now know that you can do the baby steps, and so you want to graduate up to some bigger steps, and eventually to run the course for yourself and never be weary because something inside of you tells you that you can make it.

POSTSCRIPT

YOUR CHEER SQUAD

You really must remember that the only free will that you ever have control of is your own, if people choose to come with you, they will do it of their own free will.

However, this is how a movement begins.

If it were not for political and social movements, society would be a very dull place indeed.

It is our belief that we live in a free market of ideas, and good ideas stay while bad ideas are lost with the dust of time.

If an idea is a good one, it could be a temporary change, or it could be a permanent change, so long as it is good for the social order. Now what if you believe that the social order needs to be changed, and then please change it for the betterment of all involved.

You have the power within you to change the world, but I would encourage you to please start a little closer to home, Get yourself and your own house in order before you suppose that you want to change the world. That is simply taking care of first things first, and it will prove to be the prudent way.

I now place this reasoning in your good hands as I say, "You have the power, now what are you going to do with it?"

Now we go back to the matter of the sigmoid curve. It is something called by some marketing people as the power curve. It statistically tells the observer the best time to get involved in the process.

You make money when you buy a stock at the beginning of an upswing in the market, and you sell it sometime before you think that the market is going to make the stock drop.

It is likewise with a business opportunity. You will want to get in on it at the beginning of the upward swing in the market. If you do this, you are going to get wealthy.

Social movements are no exception. The earlier you get into it, the higher you are going to go in it.

Napoleon Hill taught us that observing things, and getting into things that show you this kind of growth is the way to thinking and prosperity. If you put the thought into It, you are going to benefit over the long haul.

Just because you are growing rich does not mean that the thinking gets to stop. If you are observing that the business that you are in is starting to wane, it might just be time to think about getting into something new or bigger.

VISION TO MAKE PROVISION

Solomon told us "without a vision the people perish." The whole point of this work of ours is to help you to realize your vision, and figure out how to make it happen. Now it is a given that you have a vision, but the first work in pursuing it is to make provision for its fulfillment. Step 1 is the plan. It may be trite but plan your work and work your plan is the best advice that I have received.

As you work to make your plan, and work in your plan to realize your goal, you are making provision, and as you make provision, you are filling your cup with the water of success. Then all you really have to do is to keep with it until the success starts, and it spills out into your life. Then you give.

ENLIGHTENED WEALTH

Once you begin to see the rewards of your success in your goal, it is very important to give something back to your community, and help those who are less fortunate.

Wealth is a two-fold thing. Either you have the blessing because the higher power knows what you will do with these things, or you have the blessing to see what you will do with these things.

It is the reason that the tenth part of my capital accrual plan is to set aside money for philanthropy.

ATTITUDES

Positivity is essential in success, but it is not essential in the beginning of the process. In the beginning of the process, you need belief, and decisiveness. If you can make a decision, believe in that decision, and act upon it, then you are off to a good start, and well begun is half-done.

STRATEGIES

This is where making your plan comes into play. I do encourage you to get to work and do the study and find someone who has succeeded in the way that you propose too, and follow his or her tracks.

Success leaves trails, and you are smart to find and to follow them. The mid course correction is very important as well.

If you find that you are off course in relation to your plan, then you need to know enough in the course of this work to know that having a mindset that draws you to your goals is what we have been talking about all along.

There are evidences from recent research that tell us something that most of who heard it went," Are you kidding me?!", That is that you improve your odds of success when you band together with like-minded people who are goal seekers in their own right, in sort of a success club. We call these Dream Teams.

DREAM TEAM

It can be a success club, and entrepreneurs club, or an investors club. It is the watchword of these concepts that all those who are involved should have similar goals.

Then you are to make the team aware of and accountable for your goals, as you are to become for theirs, and then you report to each other on a periodic basis as to how you are doing, and elicit advice and input from the members.

We find that there is an eighty percent increase in the probability of achieving even greater success if you are accountable to a group. It really is a fascinating dynamic to see that there is a great power in being in a team of like-minded people. As if, we did not know.

It is most important that you be there for each other and that you.

FOLLOW THROUGH WITH EACH OTHER

It is also very important that you see that this does not need to be a solitary endeavor. It can actually be a social occasion of some merit.

There would appear to be nothing nobler than to make yourself better. It is the first step in making a better world. I cannot stress the importance to you of making your goals into a tangible part of your daily reality.

It was never the money, but the things that the money can facilitate that are what we want. I will never tell you that money is anything but a tool to facilitate your goals.

Do you remember when I told you about setting up a capital accrual program?, and that would set aside 10% of my gross to capital. Now here is why.

You want to build a portfolio of income producing assets, but ones that do not take so very much of your time. You should have things that are more important.

Buy another business, and put management in that you can trust, or buy an investment property and hire a local management company to run it.

You would really rather spend the time with your family on a beach somewhere, or running your primary business?

RELATING MY HISTORY

I have done everything:, or will soon do everything that I have told you about in this text. So you can see that in my planning, I have accounted for all of my passions, and when it comes down to it, If the worst case scenario should happen, and I could not expand beyond where I am right now, my life is still light years above where it was just 24 months ago. Therefore, I am better off just because I have walked upon this path, and I have absolutely no reason to doubt that you will come to a point where if I quit, I would always know that I had settled for less than I could be.

That would be tragic after all of the bad stuff that came before.

There is a book called The Magic of Thinking Big, and I took his advice, so I guess that I will know when I have arrived when I am cruising the lakes on my Hatteras M100 Motor Yacht, after having driven there in my Rolls. Everybody has dreams of grandeur. I am no exception.

I am more of a Chevy kind of person right now, as are most of us so there is still a good long way to go. That is okay because there is always hope as long as there is breath in the human form.

My question to you is: what things do you want to do before you die? This includes of the things that you would like to see, and do, before your pass from this mortal shell, and go to your great reward.

I want to greedily and rightfully seize every ticking moment, and never give one of them back, except for my golden bucket list dreams.

We all have our dreams, and we all have the right to seek them. We all also have the power to achieve them at any point in our lives. You can see it, you can believe it, and then there is one sure thing. I want you to come to believe, and that is the sure fact that you can achieve it . . . SRB

As I believe firmly in this work, and more importantly, as a service to you, I will make myself available to answer your specific questions.

If you need: to e-mail me personally at; srbb1959@live.com I will do my very best to answer them all, and to help you.

Acknowledgements

1) Stand on the shoulders of giants" Ref quote
   Sir Isaac Newton
2) Commencement address made by Winston
   Churchill at Harrow in 1941
3) Napoleon Hill: Think and Grow Rich
   Chapter Two
4) John Naisbitt; Megatrends 1974
5) Fight Club: Ref Fox 2000 Pictures, Regency
   Enterprises, A Linson Films Production for the chicken
   feathers quote
6) Much respect to Mr. Anthony Robbins for the concepts
   of Neuro-associative conditioning, and role modeling.
7) Robert Kyosaki: Rich Dad Poor Dad
   Ref from chapter 2
8) The Beebe Research Project including:
   Robert Burns, a.k.a. Stephen Beebe, Tony
   Cooper, Cathy Wilkinson, and Edmundo Cardenas
9) Dr. Deborah Williams

NOTES:

About The Author

Stephen R. Beebe is an insightful person who, when he had hit his bottom got other minds involved, and collectively they helped each other to build better lives.

In this book, he has revealed the process and the events that helped him to redirect his life, and to help the lives of the others in that team, and has done so with powerful brevity.

He was born in Pasadena, Ca, Raised in
Texas, Lived for years in Portland,
Oregon, and is planning a relocation back East.
He holds a Bachelors degree from
Niagara University, and is back at school
Working to become a Professor, getting an MBA, and then he would like to seek a Doctorate to teach at a University.